Dolphin Tribe

Remembering the Human-Dolphin Connection

Ashleea Nielsen

Dancing Dolphin Press

Author photo: Joe Cabebe, Kahului, HI
Interior design & copy editing: Sara Patton, Wailuku, HI

Publisher's Cataloging-in-Publication Data
(prepared by Quality Books Inc.)

Nielsen, Ashleea D.
    Dolphin tribe : remembering the human-dolphin connection /
Ashleea Dawn Nielsen.
    p. cm.
    Includes bibliographical references.
    Preassigned LCCN: 94-60064.
    ISBN 0-9637429-3-0

    1. Human-animal communication.   2. Dolphins.   I. Title.

QL776.N54 1993   591.59

                QBI93-1074

It is with great love that I dedicate

this work to all the many Kingdoms.

I honor your life and light.

Contents

Acknowledgments

For their faith, encouragement, assistance, and inspiration, my thanks to Bob Neal, Joie Shining-Star, Tom & Nancy Vendetti, and Suzanne Joyce.

I am also deeply grateful to Shirley Bliley, Horace Dobbs, Paul Forestell, Roy Goya, Mark MacKay, Sara Patton, Patsy & Lorin Stetson, and Jeri Wahinehookai.

A very special thank you to Sri Sathya Sai "Beloved" Baba. And especially, thanks to all the dolphins & whales.

Aloha!

Foreword

BY PAUL FORESTELL

HAVING STUDIED WHALES AND DOLPHINS FOR NEARLY twenty years, I have become as fascinated by the reactions these intriguing creatures evoke in humans as I am by their own unique characters. I continue to be struck by the universality with which humans are transfigured in the presence of the immensity of whales and the wizardry of dolphins. This reaction cuts across culture, age, and social status, and bespeaks an ancient and deeply entrenched connection between human and cetacean that bridges the immensity of difference between our earthbound and their waterborne existence.

Humans have interacted with whales and dolphins under many guises during recorded history. There are ancient stories of dolphins cooperating with humans to capture fish in many parts of the world; there are poetic sagas of dolphins developing friendships with children, and leading sailors out of turbulent seas. But there is also the horrendous history of human slaughter of whales using barbarous techniques, even in modern day. Needless killing of thousands of dolphins continues even as you read this. We have shown many faces to our marine cousins—and the result has seldom been flattering.

Today there is a worldwide fascination with opportunities to interact with whales and dolphins. We need to honestly ask ourselves what we are looking for in these experiences. Which face do we show the dolphins when we set out to find them in their own environment? Are we interested in the welfare of the dolphin? Or are we simply seeking some new thrill, or an escape from a world overloaded with thrills? Are we willing to take the time to learn about the other presence on which we want to impose ourselves? Are we willing to develop the sensitivity to approach our earth- and oceanmates with openness to their perceptions and their needs? Are we willing to put aside our self-centered understandings and broaden our consideration of other possibilities? Can we let ourselves be taught by them?

As we continue to explore interactions with whales and dolphins, the need will grow for wise teachers who can guide us through the intricate pathways of the human/cetacean interface. Ashleea Nielsen is one of those teachers, and it was with refreshing delight that I first picked up her book and found myself being drawn into her impressive understanding of what we need to know to better approach dolphins with openness and care. It is clear that Ashleea knows dolphins as complex marine beings with their own challenges, concerns, and strategies for survival—they are not simply swimming around in the ocean waiting to entertain humans!

Ashleea's natural history account covers an important array of helpful information in a succinct and accurate manner. But *Dolphin Tribe* does more than simply provide interesting dolphin facts. I believe it is a handbook for exploration. And it points the way to some of the most interesting terrain one could imagine.

As a scientist, there have been many times when I have come up against the dichotomy of understanding dolphins as "experimental preparations" and understanding them as creatures with minds beyond ours. In my studies of dolphin language, tests of their memory, and investigations of their sensory processes, I have tried to walk the line of scientific rigor. Nonetheless, the dolphins have continuously urged me beyond the procrustean bed of human egocentrism and into the realm of mental communion that is not possible in any other setting of which I know. The scion of cetacean/human interactions, Dr. John Lilly, has pointed out that the only evidence we have of human superiority is our own self-congratulatory claims. Communication with another species therefore becomes an important test of who we are. What will the dolphins tell us about our place on this planet when we finally learn how to listen to them? Ashleea's teaching helps prepare us for finding that answer.

Perhaps the most critical lesson I have learned from reading Ashleea's book is that the resolution of the quest to increase our knowledge of other species lies in first coming to know ourselves. The insights and exercises shared in *Dolphin Tribe* provide the promise that as we bring our own emotions, needs, and energies to a more centered place, we increase the likelihood of crossing the threshold of human limitations. The place beyond is a world of connect-edness that humans have sought to re-establish ever since primordial events set us on the path of cognitive conceit and spiritual dysfunction that we face today. *Dolphin Tribe* serves as a critical prescription for correcting that dysfunction.

We need beacons to take us through the sometimes troubled waters of dolphin attraction. We need beacons that do not constrain our path by limiting our explorations, but rather keep us off the rocks and point us to open water. Ashleea Nielsen has provided the gift of many beacons, and in so doing shows her care for humans and for dolphins; a care that is shaped by balancing the realities of human and dolphin being with the vision of soaring to a higher plane of interaction. I thank her for this gift, and invite you to step out into a universe where the only limitations are the ones you forgot to leave at the door.

PAUL FORESTELL
DIRECTOR OF RESEARCH & EDUCATION
PACIFIC WHALE FOUNDATION

Preface

AS I SIT HERE ON THIS RAINY DAY IN MAUI, I KEEP thinking about how much has changed since I first began this book three years ago. At that time, I was living in Laguna Niguel, California, a couple of miles from the ocean, and I was feeling strong inspiration to communicate what I knew and felt about cetaceans and interspecies communication. I finished the book and I put it aside. Until now . . .

For some reason there had been a lack of interest in the subject matter or in my expression of it. Nothing I said—in the book, or in conversations with others—brought much response. What's wrong with this picture? I asked myself. Why is it that editors, friends, and associates don't find dolphins and whales compelling, or the prospect of interspecies communication exciting news?

This was certainly not so for me! I could palpably feel a breakthrough coming for our battleworn planet, wherein there would no longer be any separation between species and the various tribes. Dawn was just around the corner, and I wanted to crow the news far and wide!

Perhaps I was ahead of my time then. Well, to make a long story short, I made several transformative changes in my life . . . geographically, as well as in my career, friends, and loved ones! I ended up on the Hawaiian island of Maui, with my whole life rearranged. And for the better!

Maui is considered by many to be the heart chakra of the planet, and a great place for healing. People instinctively flock here to heal and be healed.

Even the enormous humpback whales journey here to mate and give birth. They know why they come here. I knew why I came too. So do passing visitors to Maui, even if their knowledge is subconscious. Maui heals and changes you. If you want a crash course in consciousness expansion, where life is your teacher, Maui is the place!

Even with all my shifts in attitude (and latitude), I am still searching for my special tribe members. I have met many on Maui, but I know we are an even larger, farther-ranging tribe. Our nature is freedom. We are lovers of adventure and expansion.

I hope this book reaches you who belong to this tribe. If I put out the information, surely I will receive feedback from you who resonate with dolphins, whales, and the idea of interspecies communication.

How do you know if you belong to this tribe? Do dolphins and whales make your heart beat faster? Do you get a rush being in or near the ocean, "the Big Blue"? Can you communicate with all kinds of people and animals? Is freedom a big priority for you? Do you feel drawn to the starry night skies? Have you always known there are fairies and angels? Do you like to play and have fun? Are people always telling you to grow up and stop acting like a kid?

If you answered these questions with a loud YES! I would suggest that you are a member of the dolphin/whale tribe. Rediscovering this belonging will make you feel wonderful, ecstatic. Celebrate when you make the reconnection, for you have begun your journey Home.

Welcome and aloha from a fellow *dol-fun!*

ASHLEEA

Dolphin Tribe

Chapter One:
Getting Acquainted With Dolphins

Dolphins are guides to alternate realities. They are the link between the Dreamtime dwellers and the children of Earth.

I WAS GIVEN A GOLDEN OPPORTUNITY TO WORK WITH dolphins when I was twenty-one. The two dolphins I worked with were Maui, a male, and Puka, a female. I assisted the dolphin trainer. This meant I got to lug heavy pails of smelt to feed the dolphins during the day, participate in communication exercises with the dolphins, record our findings in the log, and hang out with the dolphins every day. I was in heaven! What could be more perfect, I kept asking myself, than to live in Hawai'i and have friends who were dolphins?

I had always loved dolphins, so this was a dream come true. I had dreamed of swimming and frolicking with dolphins since I was young. I grew up in the Midwest, but the ocean called me, so as soon as I graduated from a Texas university I headed West.

This was not because of ambition, but because that was where "the Big Blue" was.

When I saw the movie, *Day of the Dolphin*, I sobbed with deep sorrow I couldn't even begin to define. I talked with others who also had a powerful emotional response to the movie. It's as if we felt the dolphins were our family, and this movie reminded us of how homesick we really were. I knew I belonged with them.

It's no exaggeration to say that my days in that job were spent in bliss, as anyone who has spent time around dolphins understands. They bring a blessing with them, and I feel they opened my heart and allowed me to love. Like many, I came from a dysfunctional family, and I was definitely shut down as far as love goes. For the first time in my life I felt truly loving and loved. Looking back now, I see it was no accident that at this time in my life I fell "head over heels" in love with these magical creatures.

Each morning when I arrived at the ocean-water lagoon where the dolphins were kept, I greeted them. Sometimes they would swim over to greet me, and sometimes they were aloof. Knowing what I know

now, and feeling the way I do today, I could never endure seeing them penned up, even in an ocean-water lagoon. But back then I was ignorant of the fact that dolphins need their freedom. In fact, now I know that *freedom* and *dolphin* go together like *salt* and *pepper.*

A houseboat served as our base of operation. We used hydrophones (underwater microphones) and recording equipment to issue spoken commands to the dolphins. The task was to get the dolphins to follow various commands, which they almost always did, perfectly and precisely. The research, from my point of view, seemed to be a success, which opened up possibilities for enhanced communication between the species.

When I was hired, I was told there was a strict rule: absolutely no swimming with the dolphins! Happily, I found that stroking and playing with them at dockside satisfied my yearning for inter-action. On several occasions though, it so happened that fate pulled me into the water!

Scientists tell us that a higher level of neurological awareness is achieved when you confront a fear and conquer it. This must be what happened to me when I finally touched a dolphin's tongue. Let me tell you, dolphins have many big, sharp teeth! It took me quite a while to overcome my fear and satisfy my curiosity about the softness of a dolphin tongue. It was worth it, for this tongue was the softest, most magical thing I had ever touched.

After that experience, my world grew bigger. I felt there was nothing I couldn't do. This is what I've heard people report after they have walked over hot coals without being burned. There is a new energy released, and a transformation in the personality, through that confrontation of fear.

One day the trainer and I had a visitor at the lagoon: the eminent scientist, Dr. Batteau, who was the head of the project. He looked weary, his blue eyes ringed with red. After some chitchat, we left him standing on the dock outside and resumed our work on the log books inside the houseboat.

Suddenly we heard a splash and a cry for help. We ran outside and saw Batteau thrashing around in the water with a look of terror on his face. The dolphins were gently nudging him, and this made him even more hysterical. We quickly fished him out, a very shaken and much relieved man. Soon after this incident, I heard a radio report of his death by drowning. The research project was closed.

Exactly twenty years later, I became involved with dolphins again, but this time inadvertently. I was meditating in my desert home, as I had been doing for many years, when suddenly I found myself in a telepathic mode with a pod of dolphins. I was astonished, and I wondered if I had suddenly taken leave of my senses. It felt so real, but how could something like this happen so far away from the ocean, and for what reason? As I recall the experience now, it felt like an altered state, and I received a definite "high" from it. It took me quite a while to resume my normal state of consciousness.

The message I received came in the form of pictures, and I felt a clear "knowing" that a big change was coming for me, that I was to be moving back to Hawai'i. Shortly after this incident, I received a call from out of the blue, from an old friend inviting me to come to Hawai'i. At first I was reluctant. Arizona was my home, and a move didn't seem likely or relevant. However, through an odd combination of coincidences and events, this is indeed what took place. I sold most of my belongings, and off I went with my daughter and my girlfriend Sue, to begin another Hawaiian adventure. I didn't have a job, friends, or anything special waiting for me there. I just felt compelled to return to Hawai'i.

Even though I wouldn't have wanted to admit this to many people, I knew that the dolphins had another initiation in store for me, and that the move was definitely dolphin-connected. I wasn't sure of the details, but I understood I was being given an invitation to grow in consciousness.

I'm no stranger to the paranormal, and have had my share of visions and unexplainable events, but this time, I told myself, was really the topper. Who would believe that dolphins were talking to me in the desert?

I began searching for an answer. Of course, synchronicity was at work, and suddenly I found that books, magazine articles, and people turned up to answer my many questions. I met otherwise sane and apparently well-balanced people who told me that they too were receiving dolphin communications in the desert. Shortly thereafter, an organization was formed called Desert Dolphins.

This was indeed a turning point in my life, as

once again I realized that there was a much bigger world out there than I had supposed. I was excited to imagine the possibilities. My mind had been challenged to rethink my world and dare to dream of another one.

The idea of telepathy with dolphins intrigued me. I began suggesting to others (who were receptive) that they try this experiment: Communicate with dolphins wherever you are and see what happens. I wanted to get some feedback.

I attended a conference, and heard speakers with many different backgrounds tell stories about their own communication with cetaceans. These people were not crackpots. They were sensitive, articulate, sincere, and excited about this development in their consciousness. They talked about how the dolphins and whales were conveying all kinds of messages to them.

The dolphins' message that was the clearest and most insistent for me was: "It's time to come home." Now that can be interpreted in many different ways. Did they mean this literally, and if so, where was home? Or did they mean "home" as the place our heart is, a return to alignment with our inner being?

This was the most likely interpretation, I decided.

It was time to begin my healing work on myself, especially concerning issues of the heart. Like many others, I had put up blocks or barriers around my heart as protection from emotional pain. I am referring here to my heart chakra.

Chakras (from the Sanskrit word for "wheels") are special energy centers that exist within our subtle bodies. These centers are said to resemble whirling windmills or flowers. They take in higher energies and transmute them to a form that the human body can use. In other words, they function as energy transformers, "stepping down" a higher energy into a lower level energy that our bodies can use. There are seven main chakras within the human body, and five outside and above the body.

The fourth chakra is the heart chakra. It is found in the area directly over the heart and thymus gland. Within this chakra there are seven doors or openings. Depending on the person, each opening might be blocked, or only one or two openings might be blocked. We build these blockages ourselves, usually without conscious awareness, as a defense against emotional pain. Considering the dysfunctional society we live in, it would be safe to say that most people have *some* heart blockage.

The heart chakra is very important, in that it tells of an individual's ability to express love: both self-love and love toward others. The lessons of love are probably the most important thing we can learn during our sojourn on Earth. Inability or difficulty learning these lessons eventually affects the physical heart. It's not surprising to me that there are so many deaths from heart disease. There are many books that scientifically detail the link between a person's ability to love and heart disease.

Love can manifest in several ways: as platonic love, romantic love, unconditional love, etc. As we develop our ability to unconditionally love ourselves and others, our heart chakra begins to open, the blocks disappear, and we see the world in a different light.

Blockage of energy flow in one chakra can result in too much or too little energy flow to the other chakras, with a resulting imbalance in the entire physical system. Ultimately, emotional issues will have to be looked into and corrected for the whole system to run smoothly.

Since I began receiving these messages from the dolphins so many years ago, I've diligently worked on removing the blockages from my heart chakra. I've definitely made much progress and improvement in this area, but I'm not "home" yet! I still have to develop even more self-love. In my quest to heal myself, I've attended seminars and workshops of all kinds. I've experimented with seemingly every kind of bodywork—from rolfing to Hawaiian temple massage. I've meditated, prayed, and communed with the dolphins and whales. I've made significant shifts that are apparent to myself and others.

I am more integrated now, and feel certain that I'm on my way Home. One of these days, I'm going to click my shiny red shoes together three times, blow a kiss to the dolphins, and find myself Home at last!

Chapter Two:
Provocative Dolphin Facts

*Divine dolphin, why did you
exchange the land for the sea?*

DOLPHINS HAVE LONG ENJOYED THE REPUTATION OF being friends of humanity. They are very responsive to people's needs. For instance, there have been many reports of people who nearly drowned being pushed ashore by dolphins.

Both myths and physiological similarities suggest that we may share a genetic history. Scientifically, dolphins are classified as marine mammals within the order of Cetacea (which includes dolphins and whales). Like other mammals, cetaceans breathe air, are warm-blooded, and give birth to live young.

I believe that humans and dolphins are related, and that they are "water humans." They are thinking, dreaming, feeling, self-aware entities who are evolving just as we are.

Fossils indicate that at one time dolphins lived on

land. Perhaps a catastrophe occurred, or they ran to escape a hungry beast, or there was too much competition for food. For whatever reason, it was around fifty million years ago that their first major shift back to the sea took place.

One theory suggests that after this shift, some of the dolphins and whales decided to come back out of the sea, and they evolved into humans. This genetic connection may account for the strong telepathic rapport between humans and dolphins.

Since dolphins have finger bones inside their flippers and vestigial pelvic bones, it seems likely that they once had four limbs and moved about on land. They have adapted themselves to the ocean environment so effectively that they can, at will, turn up the heat of their body, or cool it off, by means of ingeniously designed blood vessels. Thus, they can move from tropical to arctic waters.

Much has been written about the size of a dolphin's brain, and there has been conjecture as to how intelligent they are. Still, no one knows for sure how the dolphin uses such a large brain, and research continues.

The paralimbic lobe is a unique feature of the

cetacean brain, in which all sensory and motor areas are represented. The lobe is separate, but attached. This is not found in the brain of any other mammal.

Because we do not have a paralimbic lobe, it is difficult for us to fully understand its function. It is believed to work like a computer. Information is gathered by all the senses and flashed through the paralimbic lobe. The whale or dolphin may then perceive in a single sensation that which we must learn through one-at-a-time sensations and reasoning. In other words, cetaceans may synthesize instantly and holographically information that takes us much longer to comprehend.

Their lateralized brain allows cetaceans to sleep with half their brain while the other half conducts business as usual. Aside from the need to be alert to danger, dolphins must remain at least partially awake because respiration is a consciously controlled function, not automatic as it is with humans. If a dolphin lost consciousness, it would stop breathing and drown.

The dolphin's sharpest sense is hearing, and much of its brain is involved in processing and extracting information from sound. Dolphins can detect and project ultrasonic frequencies as high as 180,000 cycles per second. That's ten times what humans can hear and project. This sonar acts like x-ray vision, so a dolphin can detect what is inside something using its echoing sound devices.

A dolphin can kill a shark by butting it with its powerful beak. By using their sonar to help them aim, they know exactly where to strike. They also use this capability to exchange information with each other and to locate food.

Dolphins are curious. They love to nuzzle and cavort and stroke each other with their flippers. They love to play.

Dolphins are highly sexual. They can get aroused by just about anything or anyone, including humans. One woman said she could always get the dolphin's attention at the petting pond at Sea World by thinking erotic thoughts! Dolphins mate as often as they want, and at any time of the year. No one knows for certain how their relationships work, but it is believed that relationships in general are greatly important to them. They form groups called pods, and it is rare to see a lone dolphin.

The bottle-nosed dolphins are well known, but

there are many other types as well: spinners, black-chins, helmets, snubfins, duskies, bridled, spotted, melon-heads, risso, peals, heavisides, hector's, white-beaks, piebald, irrawaddy, Amazon, and hourglass, to name a few.

There are ocean dolphins and river dolphins. Some dolphins prefer the deep waters of the ocean. These are the ones most often spotted riding the bow waves of boats. Others, such as the bottle-nosed dolphins, prefer the shallower waters of coastal regions and are often spotted near islands. Some prefer warm tropical waters, while others like their water chilly.

People are most familiar with bottle-nosed dolphins because they are probably the most adaptable to captivity. They are often seen in shallow water, riding the surf. I used to see them frequently in the ocean in Del Mar, California. One time, a friend jumped into the water and swam out to bodysurf with them. What a beautiful spectacle: man and dolphins "blissing out" in giant waves!

There are dolphins who live in the rivers of China, India, and Brazil. The pink dolphin of the Amazon is one of the oddest, yet most adorable dolphins. It is close to extinction because of the scoundrels who kill them and sell their eyes for good luck charms.

There is a dolphin called the narwhal that lives in the arctic waters. It has a long ivory tusk. (Some researchers believe that the legend of the unicorn sprang from this dolphin.) Their ivory tusks were valued in the Middle Ages as a remedy for poison.

Research has concluded that dolphins and whales talk to each other. Scientists are hard at work trying to decode the cetacean languages.

Many organizations conducting cetacean research—from many different angles—have sprung up in recent years. If you are scientifically inclined, the Resource Guide at the end of this book lists research organizations that accept volunteers and offer the opportunity to work on projects with the cetaceans.

Chapter Three:
Whale Wonders

The whales like to observe humans!
Why are they so curious about us?
Do they remember us?

SIZE, POWER, AND INTELLIGENCE COME TO MIND when you consider the whale, a great god swimming through the water. The largest brain ever created . . . a mouth as large as a meeting room . . . a flipper as big as an airplane wing . . . a penis eight feet long . . . these are some of the whale's amazing characteristics.

Man has hunted whales for hundreds of years. The whale meat has been used for food, the oil for light and heat (and now as lubricants for missiles), the bones for implements, the intestines for twine, and so on. For a complete list of what we've used the whale for, read *Whale Nation* by Heathcoat Williams. The pictures and verse are certain to evoke an emotional response—they did for me! This book is truly educational and enlightening.

One of my favorite whales, the humpback, was hunted to the brink of extinction. According to some figures, it is believed to be making a comeback. Today, humpback whales are an endangered species, with a worldwide population estimated at between 5,000 and 10,000.

Nowadays whales have to contend with water pollution, commercial fishing fleets taking their food, increasing ship traffic and noise, oil spills, and an abundance of whale-watching boats loaded with tourists, disturbing their privacy and solitude.

Every winter, humpbacks come to frolic and mate in the warm Hawaiian waters; in early spring they return to Alaska for the summer. Sanctuaries have been proposed where whales would be allowed to mate, calve, and feed without being disturbed by tourists or researchers. This seems like it would be ideal . . . an idea whose time has come.

Over a five-month period there are somewhere between 600 and 1,200 humpbacks, each weighing approximately 40 tons and measuring up to 45 feet long, roaming off the shores of Hawai'i, mostly near the island of Maui. Islanders can't wait for them to arrive every year. They're like family, and of course they're a prime tourist attraction.

Maybe it's because whales are similar to us (being air-breathing mammals who nurse their young), maybe it's because they show interest in us, maybe it's because they put on a fabulous show . . . *whatever* the reason, everyone wants to watch the whales. They are a show that is truly spectacular.

When you see a 40-ton giant leap skyward (known as a "breach"), it is impressive! Your impulse is to hoot and holler and pray for more. Sometimes whales breach in rapid succession, making the occasion even more joyful and exciting.

Besides the spectacular leaps, watch for their "plumes" or gushes of spray, which are simply the humpback's lungs expelling air. These plumes rise up to a mist 10 to 20 feet high, a pretty sight to view on a beautiful Hawaiian morning.

If you're lucky enough to be underwater, you may hear one of the hauntingly beautiful humpback "whale songs." The songs change every year and are eerie. They are a complex multilayered series of frequencies that sound like high shrieks, birds chirping, low rumbles—even angels singing, according to some imaginative listeners.

The songs carry for a long distance underwater. There are many tapes of these songs available, some mingled with jazz and/or other animal voices in concert. (The Resource Guide at the end of this book lists some of my favorites.)

Humpbacks begin to sing just before or during migration to the breeding grounds, and continue to sing through the breeding season. It is always a lone male who does the singing.

In my opinion, singing is the wrong word for it. I believe they are talking, communicating, perhaps commanding. This is communication of the highest order, just like our own human language.

When did humpback whales begin talking? A long, long time ago. Only recently have we begun to listen. It wasn't until World War II that we began systematically listening to underwater sounds. During this time, the Navy set up stations to listen for approaching enemy submarines. Very soon there were reports of unidentified sounds.

After the war, a hydrophone was developed that enabled scientists to better study these sounds. In 1952 a published report announced the discovery of whale songs and created public awareness.

Researchers theorize that the male sings to lure and seduce the female. Perhaps he is saying, "Hey baby, come to me." It is believed there are songs for other purposes as well: to maintain contact when out of sight, in socialization activities, and dialogues during feeding. It has also been suggested that there may be regional dialects as well as individual and unique signatures to each humpback voice pattern.

Several years ago, I had a vivid vision as I was drifting off to sleep. I saw an ancient, wrinkled whale eye looking at me. It was huge. I received the impression that the consciousness behind this eye felt great compassion for me. I was immediately swept into a rush of Pure Love. Suddenly a laser-like red beam shot from this eye to my forehead. I felt as if I had been zapped by powerful energy! I was elated. Since this experience, I have become increasingly aware of whales and their profound energy.

Grey whales are considered the "friendlies" because they have shown great curiosity about humans for years. These barnacle-encrusted knobby-faced giants like to swim up to whale-watching boats and check out everyone on board.

Every year between December and March, they make their way down the California coastline to a place in Baja California called Laguna San Ignacio, to breed and calve. And every year tourists crowd on to boats in all kinds of weather, just to catch sight of their flukes and maybe have an opportunity to pet one of these ugly-but-cute whales on its head and upper jaw. There is a term to describe the whale poking its head out of water to inspect the people on a boat: *spyhopping,* or, as the old whalers used to term it, *pitch-poling.*

What are the whales looking for? They are supposed to have fairly good eyesight. Are they merely curious? Perhaps they are transmitting something to the passengers with their eyes (like in my vision).

Several years ago I attended an event called "The Underwater Photographer's Film Festival," which for several nights showed underwater pictures and films made by divers. Held in San Diego and hosted by Jean Michel Cousteau, it was attended by approximately 6,000 enraptured viewers. People were literally standing in the aisles. I was awestruck at such a turnout! Our population has an incredible *longing* to learn about the ocean and its inhabitants.

I believe the ocean, whales, and dolphins are calling us.

Come home, they are whispering. *Remember . . .*

Chapter Four:
Dolphin Swimming
& Dreaming

*No animal figures more prominently in
Greek and Roman myths than the dolphin.
It represents the powerful gods themselves.
Dreaming of dolphins signifies good.*

Swimming

Swimming with dolphins has become a major tourist attraction. At the Hyatt Waikoloa on the Big Island in Hawai'i, there are so many people who wish to have the experience of swimming with the dolphins (in an enclosed setting) that the hotel uses a lottery system to select the lucky participants. On the other hand, if you're unlucky enough to be spotted swimming with the dolphins (or whales) in the open oceans of Hawai'i, you'll be fined. The authorities don't want people disturbing the local dolphins or whales.

But don't despair. There are a multitude of individuals and groups that offer the dolphin encounter in many different parts of the world . . . the Bahamas, the Florida Keys, near Gibraltar, the Mediterranean,

New Zealand, South America, the United Kingdom, the Turks, the Providentiales, the Caicos Islands, and Tenerife.

*Those who have swum with dolphins, either
in roped-off enclosures or in the open ocean,
have reported themselves changed in some way.
They say the experience is exhilarating. They
report physical changes and healings. They
feel more childlike and creative. The impact of
the experience stays with them for a long time.
They want to swim with the dolphins again
and again!*

Along with many other dolphin experts, I believe
that it's a potentially dangerous situation for dolphins to be confined in an enclosure with people
they might not like, where the dolphin has no option
of escaping. A dolphin that weighs between 250 and
425 pounds is nothing to fool with! Dolphins have
their likes, dislikes, moods, good days, and bad days,
just as we do! I believe that it's preferable for people
to swim in areas that are not confined—the "wild"—

because this allows the dolphin a choice of whether to approach or not.

There is a growing field of research with dolphins and autistic children. Many of these children have spoken for the first time after spending time in the water with the dolphins. All of the autistic children who swam with the dolphins were positively affected in some way. For this situation, enclosed pools are the best location. The dolphins seem willing to be with these children; I feel they probably "volunteered" for their teaching post.

Dr. Igor Charkovsky of the Soviet Union has assisted in the births of many human babies in the Black Sea, with a pod of dolphins swimming nearby. Their presence seems to comfort and relax the mothers during childbirth. Some say that these babies are strongly telepathic, and that as they grow up they return to the Black Sea year after year to be greeted by the same dolphins who attended their birth.

Organizations & Projects

Some of the projects available to those who want to swim and communicate with dolphins follow.

(Addresses are in the Resource Guide at the end of this book.)

THE WILD DOLPHIN PROJECT, in existence since 1985, studies the communication and social systems of a group of free-ranging spotted dolphins in the Bahamas. Members of the public are invited in small groups to assist in the field research and swim with dolphins.

OCEANIC SOCIETY EXPEDITIONS offers a variety of workshops all over the world. One such offering is a week-long trip to the Amazon on the 36-passenger riverboat *Arca*. The workshop covers the triumphs and challenges of dolphin and whale conservation, and reviews current river dolphin research efforts. There are daily excursions by small skiffs to observe and record pink river dolphins and the tiny acrobatic tucuxi dolphins. You can also join an expedition to Belize, Hawai'i, Nepal, or the Bahamas to research dolphins.

EARTHWATCH is a tax-exempt institution that

sponsors scientists, artists, teachers, and students in documenting a changing world. Their projects with the whales and dolphins are extensive.

JOAN OCEAN'S DOLPHIN CONNECTION offers a six-day experience with the dolphins in the Hawaiian waters near the Big Island. Along with her staff, she teaches "how to communicate with dolphins and other multi-dimensional beings, and how to apply these new paradigms of life to ourselves every day."

DOLPHINSWIM is directed by Rebecca Fitzgerald, who takes small groups of people to swim with a pod of wild spotted dolphins off the Bahama islands. Some of these trips are joined by other dolphin experts, including Dr. Horace Dobbs, Dr. Masato Nakagawa, and Timothy Wyllie. Rebecca is currently exploring the possibility of starting a Bahama Dolphin Retreat Center.

DOLPHINS PLUS is located in Key Largo, Florida, along with the Environmental Research and

Educational Foundation. They operate a marine mammal facility involved in environmental education programs, in-water therapeutic encounters with dolphins for special needs children, and the study of interspecies interaction between dolphins and humans.

Their educational programs are designed for those interested in learning more about dolphins and their environment, and they provide a total role reversal experience, with the human entering the dolphin's world as a swimmer or snorkeler. These programs are held twice daily, where a limited number of humans go into the water with the dolphins.

Dolphins Plus also offers field trips to the offshore reefs and the Everglades. They emphasize that they are a serious research and educational facility, not an amusement park.

PRESERVATION OF THE AMAZON RIVER DOLPHIN was founded by Roxanne Kremer. This organization takes people on trips to the Amazon River to see the pink dolphin. They also focus on conservation of the jungles of

Peru and Brazil. You can adopt a dolphin and/or an acre of rainforest for a small contribution.

THE INTERNATIONAL CETACEAN EDUCATION RESEARCH CENTRE (ICERC) is scheduled to be built in Australia, where interdisciplinary research and study of dolphins and whales can be combined for the first time.

The founder, Kamala Hope-Campbell, feels that the dolphins and whales have excellent communication skills—superior to our language and skills—that they can teach us.

THE UNDERWATER EXPLORERS SOCIETY (UNEXSO) calls their program The Dolphin Experience. They have a group of Atlantic bottle-nosed dolphins in residence at their facility in the Bahamas. They are training these dolphins to be released into the ocean daily, to swim freely with scuba divers on the coral reef. You can register for their one-, two-, or five-day trainer program, where you will assist the trainers with all aspects of the dolphin program.

DOLPHIN DISCOVERY TOUR offers you eight days in the Bahamas and in the Florida Keys. "From swimming with dolphins to metaphysical coursework to scuba certification and/or sleeping in an undersea lodge, this vacation offers something for all of us who seek the thrill of ocean exploration, to discover more about ourselves and our world."

THE DOLPHIN RESEARCH CENTER houses its dolphins in natural saltwater lagoons with a low fence separating them from the sea. They offer "A Dolphin Encounter," which includes a thirty-minute orientation, an educational walking tour of the facility, the swim itself, and a thirty-minute final workshop and discussion. They also offer "Dolphinsight," a half-day program that includes a guided tour of the facility, open-air workshops on specifics of dolphin physiology and their world of sound, conservation issues, and the dynamics and philosophies of training. Working with an experienced trainer, you will have the opportunity to touch and communicate with the dolphins through verbal and hand signals. You can also spend a week with them in their Dolphinlab program, getting hands-on experience and education.

**KAIKOURA TOURS** is located in New Zealand, where dusky dolphins, known for their boisterous behavior and spectacular leaps, are close to shore from October through May. You can snorkel among them. Kaikoura also offers seal swimming tours, dive tours, and sperm-whale-watching. The sperm whale is the largest of all the toothed whales, and is present all year round.

**THE DANCING DOLPHIN INSTITUTE** is an ecstatic mystery school utilizing the cetacean species as a mentor, model, and metaphor, thus allowing re-emergence into loving awareness, higher consciousness, and interspecies communication. Dolphin consciousness and dolphins themselves are the teachers, with the institute staff working as facilitators. The institute is planning its first event (Initiation, Level 1) for May 1995.

Dreaming

Dreamtime journeys are different than the dreams we experience at night. The Dreamtime is a parallel universe that we reach through out-of-the-body journeying. It is the place where our soul or spirit resides, and it is unlimited.

In this place, you can do things you normally can't do in your waking reality—like triple somersaults in the air, walking through walls, or swimming underwater without scuba gear. Often, it looks identical to your normal surroundings. The reason it's so powerful is that it contains information and answers that help you be more aware and conscious in your everyday life.

Many people have the ability to access this Dreamtime reality. Some have a natural ability to arrive there, many others can be trained. The dolphins are the master teachers, and they are delighted to show us how to enter these realms. The exercises described in Chapter Six can be very helpful in this area.

Entering the Dreamtime can be accomplished in the comfort of your own home. It's important that you take precautions against being disturbed while you're traveling. If you're startled or disturbed in any way while you're out-of-body, it can be very hard on the physical body.

The dolphins are also entering our sleeptime dreams and meditations and giving us messages and information. I have heard many reports of this, and I feel that these visitations are occurring more frequently because of the dolphins' strong desire to "wake us up." I've also heard the theory that this "stepped-up" contact is caused by our exit from the third dimension and entry into the fourth and fifth dimensions.

As we stand on the verge of a major paradigm shift, the dolphins are offering to teach us, and to guide us into a more complex, yet interconnected, energetic-field-like universe. This is their universe. They are making themselves available both in our current physical reality (i.e., the proliferation of dolphin-swim tours) and in the Dreamtime.

Chapter Five:

Tuning In To Dolphins & Whales

The formula is simple: Breathe deeply, relax, and imagine tuning a radio dial until you locate the right station. You will sense it immediately . . . it sounds and feels joyful.

FOR THOSE WHO WISH TO TUNE INTO THE UNSEEN world, there is a lot of information out there. There are certain geographical places on this planet Earth (or the name I prefer: Terra) that are vortex locations. These special locations are superb places for *listening;* they are especially helpful and powerful.

Vortexes are highly sensitive areas that function very much like chakras do in the human body. They're the places where the planet "breathes" (takes energy in and releases it). The vortexes spin to balance the intake and outtake of energy. They form a great global matrix.

Because human interaction in these special areas greatly affects the world, healing thought and prayer in these places will be especially beneficial in assisting our planet through its present crisis.

There are vortexes situated all over the planet. Two famous ones are Sedona, Arizona; and Glastonbury, England. Other locations are Haleakala, Lake Titicaca, Uluru (Ayres Rock), Gunung Agung, Mount Kailas, Mount Shasta, Palenque, Mount Fuji, Tongariro, The Great Pyramid, and Table Mountain. There is believed to be a vortex that's opening in Russia in the 1990s. Vortexes can move, and it is likely that many new vortexes will be functioning in the 22nd century.

Interdimensional doorways are discovered, often quite by accident, at these sites. There are frequent reports from people winding around Glastonbury Tor that as they hike up the hill, they enter "pockets of time" where they either go back in time or fast forward into the future.

When you arrive at one of these vortex areas, find a quiet, unspoiled place ... away from the hustle and bustle, people, and electromagnetic pollution. Park yourself there.

The next step is to quiet yourself, using whatever method works best for you. Stop the thought processes in your mind until you are calm and centered. Then listen! Your soul group wants to speak to you.

The dolphins want to speak to you. Some of the information may come in loud and clear, while some may be fainter—just like radio stations when you attempt to tune them in on your radio. If you are prepared and willing, relaxed and focused, then you may tune into the cetacean channel. You don't even have to be near the water!

Just as a radio has many stations to choose from, when you decide in "tune in" there are many stations available to you. It's your *intent* that helps you focus on one particular station. And just like some stations have a very broad, powerful signal, the dolphins have a very powerful signal these days. That's why so many people are suddenly listening to "the dolphin station." The dolphins are communicating with more intensity now because it is *time!*

Time and space are not exactly what we've been taught or programmed to believe they are. Our basic consensus reality is that we live in linear time (i.e., past, present, future). However, the new physics as well as the ancient shamanistic belief system is that there are many realities, and that many of them are simultaneous.

This concept can be very disturbing to many of

us who have been living in linear reality. It's hard to imagine "no time" or "multidimensional awareness." However unfamiliar it is to us, and hard for us to believe, this concept is what I feel will ultimately become our consensus reality.

You can send a message or image to anyone or anything on this planet, and to other dimensions or planets. We are all interconnected in the web of life. Through this web that connects us, we can know beyond ourselves. The cetaceans are masters of knowing. And we can be too, with practice.

Have you heard that we're shifting from the third dimension to the fifth dimension? Are you wondering exactly what that means? There are many prophets and futurists trying to explain what this world will be like when we no longer have only a limited third-dimensional existence, but instead function from the expansiveness of the fifth dimension.

I believe that the most noticeable change will be that we will no longer feel separate from others. We will experience the energy flow that connects us with each other, and with other species.

The dolphins wish to reconnect with us now.

It's time for a family reunion! They have patiently waited for us to remember who we are and experience "group mind." This is the ability to process information instantly, without third-dimensional technological hardware. It implies increased awareness on every level, and full remembrance that we are part of the ALL.

Some people believe that certain dolphins have "shape-shifted" (changed form) through the ages and visited humans as famous illumined personages such as Jesus and Buddha. Supposedly, dolphins have been guiding our evolution here on Terra.

In metaphysical literature, Sirius, a double-star system, is reputed to be the original home of the cetaceans. Sirius, also called The Dog Star, is a member of the constellation Canis Major and is 8.7 light years from Earth. It is the second nearest star and the brightest visible from Earth. As one story goes, the god-like beings that came to Earth chose to incarnate in the cetacean form because it felt more comfortable and a closer fit to their nature.

Another theory is that the whales and dolphins originated on the Pleiades. This cluster of stars — 400 light years from Earth, in the constellation

Taurus—is deeply embedded in the world's history, poetry, and mythology of the heavens. Many ruins, scriptures, and archaeological discoveries suggest that we have been visited in the past by a more advanced or evolved society.

It's hard to say for certain at the present, but it's most likely that an intergalactic mixing of species has taken place. Maybe, one of these days very soon, we will finally discover the truth about these early colonizations on Earth and fill in the missing pages of our history books.

The cetaceans are masters of communication, and they know the complete past as well as probable futures. In fact, they are giant "swimming encyclopedias."

The cetaceans are returning to our awareness in many ways . . . often tragically, such as dolphins in driftnets and beached whales. They wish to remind us to open our hearts to all the life forms on this planet.

They speak to us using the universal language of telepathy or nonverbal communication. Telepathy is more than mere thought transference. A whole host of sensations and levels of knowing can accompany telepathic communication.

All of us are telepathic. (Children and animals are especially so.) Some of us have just let our telepathic "muscle" grow weak through lack of use. But even if this is the case, the muscle can be exercised and activated should the desire or need arise. For many, this may indeed come to pass in the days ahead. Telepathy may be vital to our survival.

There are many "sensitives" who can communicate with animals. And there are a growing number of so-called "normal" people worldwide who are reporting communications from cetaceans. At a conference in Sedona, Arizona, several years ago, I heard many people describe their experiences and information they had received from the dolphins. These people were not crazy, fanatical, or eccentric. They had simply tuned in.

The question I am most often asked is: "How do the dolphins or whales communicate to you?" I receive impressions of pictures. Some of these pictures are quite silly, sometimes they are literal, at other times they are symbolic.

At one time I conducted classes to facilitate others in opening up to communication with dolphins. We

would clear ourselves and I would lead a guided
visualization into the dolphin Dreamtime. After the
visualization, class members shared their experiences.
It was amazing to hear some of the pictures that
were described. Stories were told of unusual opera-
tions performed by the dolphins, underwater caves
and temples where the Queen of the Dolphins
resides, touching (slipping, sliding) movements that
were very sensual, wide-screen television that
showed future events, and discourses and conversations with specific dolphin guides. These narrations
of the experiences were inevitably full of joy. They
also convinced me that the dolphins have a great
sense of humor and love to play!

It can be very surprising to receive telepathic
communication from another species. Yet many
people have experienced this, and so can you!

A psychic told me I would be inspired to write
this book by a dolphin who lives in the waters near
Laguna Beach—before I even moved there! When
I *did* move there, my home was several miles inland.
I feel it was actually a *pod* of dolphins that inspired
me telepathically. Whenever I visit my Dreamtime
state with the dolphin, I converse with a pod.

Telepathy is easier when you are relaxed and focused. (Exercises and suggestions for communicating with cetaceans are given in Chapter Six.) When the messages come, find time to record them, no matter how vague or dreamlike they are. Documenting them helps refresh your memory and gives you new perceptions that come with hindsight. The messages you receive may be simple. They may have nothing whatever to do with dolphins or important events. Some people receive beautiful philosophical transmissions; others receive simple directives.

A pioneer in out-of-body experience and research is Robert Monroe. Through his own out-of-body experiences and the research he has conducted in his laboratory at the Monroe Institute, he has concluded that most intelligent species use nonverbal communication. He states that it's more than what we normally term telepathy, something far more profound. He feels that humans must be able to communicate this way (using nonverbal communication) before we can associate with other intelligent species.

Imagine, if you will, the accumulated experience and knowledge the cetacean species has stored while evolving for roughly 55 million years. They have been around a lot longer than humans! Imagine the human species finally being able to access this information and learn from it. What a giant leap we would make in our evolution!

I have many friends with psychic talents, and I have been told many things. I have learned that even the best of psychics is accurate no more than 80% of the time. This is because we live in a malleable universe, one that we often rearrange and mold to our thoughts, feelings, and beliefs.

Channeling has been around for as long as humans have sought the meaning of life. Ancient shamans and prophets were the forebears of today's channels. Channels attest to receiving information from spirit guides, angels, higher selves, nature spirits, UFOs and their occupants, ascended masters, deceased humans, beings from Inner Earth, and whales and dolphins! We live in a world of many mansions. And it would seem that everyone wants to communicate!

Some of these channels are quite astonishing in their ability to command a huge auditorium with their powerful charisma. Some are believable. Some are outright charlatans who possess the Trickster energy. It is wise to be discerning and consider no one else's truth (no matter *who* they claim to be!) to be more valuable than your own.

Who knows?! Everyone thinks they do. The best approach is to develop your intuition and guidance. Trust that truth. Find a little time to be quiet and listen to the voice within. It just takes practice and confidence.

I have witnessed all kinds of channels. But none of them are as valid for me as what I receive from my own inner guidance.

As in any field, there are those who will try to use their powers to control and manipulate. In the future, I feel we will be able to actually see the aura that surrounds the body, and perceive someone's true intent. Today the aura is only visible to some. Dishonesty and trickery will become things of the past when we all develop this ability to see the truth.

These days it seems like everyone is doing what I just did . . . predicting the future! As the year 2000 approaches and the world astounds us with remarkable changes, the "prediction game" seems to be the most popular game on Earth.

Some of these predictions are gloomy and frightening. Others are optimistic. For example, the Worldwatch Institute, after warning people about environmental degradation for the last 16 years, has drafted an uncharacteristically positive blueprint for achieving a sustainable global economy within the next 40 years. By the year 2030, they foresee a world with widespread recycling, a declining birth rate, and solar thermal power replacing oil, natural gas, and coal. More people will be staying home and working out of their homes. The automobile will be almost completely replaced by mass transit and bicycles. The autos that remain will get 100 (or more) miles per gallon of fuel.

However, in its 11th annual "State of the World" report on global environmental and social conditions, Worldwatch suggests that hungry times may be ahead due to Third World population explosions, suddenly skyrocketing world rice prices, billions of acres of rangeland being chewed down to uselessness, global water shortages, and increasing fish prices. This is bad news for those who are already struggling with starvation and malnutrition.

My first experience with channeling was with Mafu. He is affectionately known as "the poor man's Ramtha," since he charges very little for his lectures. Penny Torres, the woman who channels Mafu, is a seemingly typical California girl with a "Valley-girl" vocabulary. Before she began, she told us how frightened she had been when she first saw Mafu in a physical way, and how she had since grown as a channel.

She became quiet and began touching various chakras or energy points on her body. In a couple of minutes there arose a most unusual character, one who acted quite differently than Penny. Mafu stretched as if he were Rip Van Winkle finally awakened. He began to march around the audience with a glint in his eye and an amused expression, marveling at everything he saw.

He seemed to know the secret lives of everyone he spoke to in the audience; he also knew how to "push their buttons." He had a very emotional effect on them. Many people began to cry.

Finally it was time for Mafu to speak to me. The moment he came into my presence, I froze. His energy was very unusual.

I felt like a little chameleon I had caught once in Hawai'i; it was so frightened that it switched from emerald green to pale white in an instant. After I released it, it quickly regained its original color. At the moment Mafu turned his gaze upon me, I knew exactly how that chameleon felt.

Mafu told me I had been alive 14½ million years before I came to Earth. Where does he get his figures? I wondered. He said I was to become a master. Then he spoke of the dolphins. He said they were on their last cycle on this planet, and that they had come here from another galaxy, long ago. He said they were soon to return home, as I was.

Since that first communication, I have heard other channels repeat the same idea: The dolphins are preparing for "group mind" to be established on Earth, at which time their mission will be accomplished and they will return home. The channels predict that this will happen in the not-too-distant future. They state that a major transformation is in the process of happening to the entire planet and its inhabitants. If this information is correct, and there are certainly many indications that it is, then how do we prepare? What can we do?

Chapter Six:
What To Do!

Invitations to transform have been sent. Have you received yours yet?

I RECENTLY HEARD SOMEONE QUIP: "HEY EVERYBODY, the party's moved down the hall to Room 5D!" How true. All of the fun and excitement is in our new expansion from the third and fourth dimensions into the fifth. The fifth dimension is characterized by feelings of unconditional love, peace, positiveness, unity, and a sense of responsibility for your actions because you know yourself to be the creator. We are also experiencing a shift into a light body, a subtle body that is superconscious. It resembles the physical body to some degree, but since it operates at a different energy frequency it's usually invisible to those beings operating from third-dimensional consciousness.

This is the direction we are heading toward. Some people may want to resist. But I believe that most of us know this is the next adventure, and are anticipating the growth we will experience.

How can we prepare? The following list contains qualities and skills that I feel will be essential in this time of transition.

How to Participate in Earth's "Coming-Out Party"

1. Drink lots and lots of water. This is necessary with the new frequencies accelerating.

2. Exercise and develop your telepathic abilities. Practice with your family, friends, and pets.

3. Love yourself. Accept yourself. Look into your own eyes in the mirror each day and beam the message: *I love you!*

4. Give up all excess baggage, physical and psychological. Lighten up in every way.

5. Be kind to one another. Cooperate.

6. Ask for guidance when in doubt. Ask your guardian angel, spiritual guides, your higher self, or the dolphins. It will be given.

7. Remember your greater purpose. Wake up. Team up with friends and act as alarm

clocks for each other in case sleep (amnesia) sets in again, as it is wont to do.

8. Make gratitude your attitude. The simplest and most powerful two-word prayer there is: ***Thank you.***

9. Examine your habits and correct them if needed.

10. Swim, dance, run . . . anything that makes you breathe deeply!

11. Take responsibility for your thoughts. Take responsibility for every creation in your life. Know yourself to be the master creator you truly are.

12. Radiate love and compassion.

13. Express the full range of your creativity.

14. Rejoice at your own and others' transformations.

15. Be totally who you are.

16. Expand your senses into the non-physical world. Access multiple dimensions. Tune into different stations. Explore!

17. Eliminate what causes stress for you.

18. Be a positive example to others.

19. Release all of your judgments. Monitor yourself frequently to make sure they have been released.

20. Become involved in exciting new projects . . . there will be many of them.

21. Have fun! Play together!

22. Allow yourself to feel the wonderment of a child.

How to "Tune In" To Dolphins & Whales

One of the skills that will become increasing relevant, even necessary, is telepathy. We need to break out of our isolation as a species and involve ourselves in interspecies communication.

We can begin by practicing visualization. This powerful tool has just recently been rediscovered in the West. Shamans have been using visualization since prehistory, and it has been an important part of such traditions as Taoism, tantra, siddha, and yoga.

There are plenty of books available on the subject. This technique is employed by successful individuals of diverse backgrounds. It is often used by psychologists, therapists, healers, and even the

U.S. Marines!

Creative visualization works. I know from my own experience. I've also learned that patience and trust are very much part of the process. Once you've planted the seed (visualized an idea) and watered it (put strong feelings behind it), you must wait while it grows. You have to release the idea and let it grow on its own, just as if you planted a seed in the ground. And there is just no guessing when some of those seeds you've planted will manifest.

If you would like to touch in to the dolphin energy, I offer you two visualizations. They bring rejuvenation, answers to questions, new information, and most importantly, a sense of aliveness and well-being.

If you have never tried visualizing before, the most important thing to remember is *RELAX!* Do whatever feels natural and will help you relax . . . a hot bath, a massage, or maybe just closing your eyes in your favorite easy chair.

When you are ready to begin, take your phone off the hook. Put your pets in another room. Make yourself completely comfortable and let your imagination take you on a voyage of discovery.

Preparation for Exercises

Visualize a golden light surrounding your body. Start at your left shoulder and move the light around to the other side until you feel completely enveloped and filled with this warm soothing light. Float in it. Enjoy it. Relax every muscle of your body, knowing that you are totally safe and protected within this circle of light.

Dolphin Exercise One

Do the preparation for exercises just described. Now imagine yourself standing at the top of a huge cliff. Look over the edge. Way, way down at the bottom is water. That is your destination. Waiting there for you is a pod of loving dolphins. They form a circle for you to splash down into.

Jump! Your body is as light as a feather as you slowly spiral downward. You are perfectly safe. Look at the cliff as you descend and note the layers of different ages. You are passing through history to no-time. You are returning to the center, the source, the wellspring. You are going Home.

As you approach the dolphins, visualize their excitement at your imminent arrival. See them leaping with joy. Feel their joy. Feel your joy. Gently splash down.

All is safe and well because the dolphins are encircling you. Play with them. Jump. Frolic. Allow every emotion to surface. If tears come, allow them. Whatever comes into your mind, examine it with no judgment.

Allow your childlike nature to rule. Swim. Splash. Fly. Do anything you wish. In this magical realm you can do it all. If you have any questions of your dolphin pod, formulate the question in a picture. What pictures and sensations do you receive in response?

Thank the dolphins. Immerse yourself in the loving consciousness that is present and available.

When you feel filled to the brim with vital energy and insights, say goodbye and begin your return to normal consciousness. See yourself as a mighty hawk circling upward. Take your time. Feel your radiant health and well-being.

Land on the cliff. Stretch. Trust that the information and experiences you were given were appropriate for your growth, happiness, and spiritual understanding. Write it down.

Whenever I do this exercise, I return feeling totally rejuvenated! I take these vacations frequently. They are great "stress-busters." In this dimension, I solve problems, receive answers to questions, imagine all kinds of things I'd like to manifest, and generally improve my attitude.

I have discovered that this dimension is very powerful. At first the visions may seem strange, perhaps even disturbing. But as you grow more comfortable in this space, they will delight and enlighten you. Very often these visions have a tremendous impact, and the seeds planted there come to manifestation on this plane.

I have received a wide array of pictures in this dimension. Some really made me laugh! For instance, when I was being warned of deception, I was shown the dolphins wearing little shark masks!

I feel totally protected and have explored many issues in this dimension that might have been painful to deal with normally. I feel the love of the dolphins and share with them a joyous feeling of aliveness.

Dolphin Exercise Two

This exercise is best in a swimming pool, lake, or ocean. If no body of water is available, use your bathtub and your imagination. It is preferable to be alone and undisturbed.

Relax. Do the preparation for exercises described on page 68.

Stand waist deep in the water and begin letting your body speak. Let whatever sounds that want to be released express themselves. You may feel like groaning, sighing, singing, laughing, or crying! Allow this until you feel the last bit of tension leave.

Dive into the water. Swim underwater for as long as you can. When you come up and take in the new air, imagine all your problems, sorrows, and pain leaving; and healing energies entering your body. Imagine yourself as a powerful, free, sleek dolphin. Feel this strongly.

Imagine a dolphin friend swimming beside you and pacing you. Visualize what it is you wish to know or create. Ask your dolphin friend to assist you.

If you want a problem solved, ask for a picture of a perfect resolution. If you wish to manifest something, visualize the completed fantasy in every picture-perfect detail.

You will receive the help you ask for—maybe not immediately, but often in some very astonishing ways.

This exercise is quite physical, so if you're not in good shape, don't push yourself too hard at first. I guarantee that if you continue doing this exercise, you will eventually get in great shape—in more ways than just physical. The results of this exercise are often very dramatic!

Visions

A vision is an inspired revelation. It is different than a journey into Dreamtime, or the pictures I get while meditating. Visions come to me unbidden. They come on *their* timetable, not mine. (I wouldn't know how to make a vision happen!) A vision is spectacular and showstopping. It takes you by surprise.

A vision rockets me out of my normal daily consciousness and into a big event that always leaves me amazed and stunned. Whew! What was that? Whoa, another vision! I don't always know what to make of my visions. They always seem important and meaningful, and they can always be interpreted in many different ways.

Often a vision comes when I'm relaxed, having fun, and not thinking about anything in particular. One day I was on a small boat with friends near the Hawaiian island of Lana'i (a small island near Maui). We had snorkeled, laughed, and lunched. Toward the end of the day, as the boat was cruising by high cliffs, I looked up and suddenly perceived a group of male sentinels, solemnly standing near the edge of the cliffs. They were facing out to sea, and seemed to be guarding the place. They wore tall, plumed head-gear (like that often depicted in pictures of ancient Hawaiian warriors). They were each holding a long spear or lance of some kind. I felt their impact, then suddenly was back in my normal consciousness, as the scene disappeared.

So it is with visions. They come sometimes uninvited and offer an exciting new perspective. Since dolphins are the guides to the Dreamtime, I feel sure that they participate in these "outbursts": break-throughs or sudden leaps into another conscious-ness. The dolphins probably get a good laugh out of our roller coaster ride.

I am deeply drawn into the mystery and power of these visions. They excite me. Here are some others I've experienced:

1. A new species is born worldwide, and eventually becomes dominant on Earth. The species embarks on an exploration of stars and multi-universes.

2. The world landmasses take on new shapes. California becomes a series of islands.

3. A new world headquarters is established on a landmass not visible at present. Earth and its inhabitants "graduate" to become members of the Galactic Family.

4. Space travel is accomplished using a technology that involves teleportation. Space travel includes interdimensional travel.

5. Another gender appears. It is not male or female; it is androgynous.

6. Huge space colonies orbit Earth. There are massive underwater cities too.

7. The priorities placed on food and sex change. Food is very basic, but nourish-

ing. Animal flesh and byproducts are not eaten.

Sex does not take place as frequently, yet it takes on much deeper significance. This new framework, plus new technology, extends the sexual union for several hours.

8. Death becomes a personal decision. When one decides to leave, the body is gently and easily shed. The pain and fear surrounding death are things of the past.

9. Hospitals are not necessary. The responsibility for balancing the body is up to each individual. Imbalances are noticed and corrected right away.

10. New colors are seen; new sounds are heard. All senses expand. We are able to project our thoughts and artistic creations onto a television-like screen.

Chapter Seven:
Captive Dolphins, Captive Humans

*What do the dolphins and whales want
from us to support their mission?*

I HAVE BEEN TROUBLED ABOUT THE DOLPHINS AND whales for many years. Every time I pick up mail from my box, I am reminded by the many cards and letters I receive from various organizations (many of whom are listed in the Resource Guide at the end of this book) that the situation is still desperate. These messages tell of the tragedy that is ongoing for the cetaceans. Even though many tuna manufacturers have stopped hunting the tuna that also brought dolphins up in their nets, many others are still killing dolphins in their tuna hauls. Driftnets laced across the oceans are still trapping and drowning whales and dolphins. Plastic materials take a toll on marine life. Certain countries won't abide by the international whale treaties. And on and on it goes.

These admirable organizations are in desperate

need of funds to carry on their work to save the oceans and its inhabitants. They are reaching out and asking us to unite in consciousness and action to prevent countries and organizations less concerned with our future (and our children's future) from ruining things for us all. Dramatic events result. Whaling ships are sunk! Protest marches, letter-writing campaigns, conferences with international figures are called to address the issue.

There *is* another way. Though not as obvious, it is no less active. Though extremely simple, it *is* valid. We can help shift the current reality, and assist in the Earth's transformation and divine awakening, by acting with kindness to each other and to every living creature with which we interact. We can send our healing and loving thoughts and prayers to the world. We can tune in to the dolphins and whales and tell them we love them.

As for captive dolphins and whales, they're another story. There are differences of opinion on this subject. Some say that the dolphins who are captured and end up in dolphinariums and other facilities have "volunteered" to do so. The thinking for this argument is that the dolphin "group soul" is reaching out to touch humans and interact with the human energy field, as well as introduce people to dolphin consciousness. And this proximity to humans, albeit one of imprisonment, is the method some dolphins are choosing.

In many ways these captive dolphins may be experiencing more freedom than their human counterparts. The dolphins are probably going out-of-body all the time. They are probably soaring through the multi-dimensions and laughing all the way, wishing we could play with them more.

Others argue that these highly intelligent and altruistic beings are being held against their will in overcrowded prisons, where they are subjected to all sorts of adverse conditions such as infected water, chlorine poisoning, heart failure attributable to stress, and attacks by other dolphins due to over-crowding. This theory suggests that no amount of fun or education for humans could ever justify what we are doing by incarcerating these beings.

I have made visits to captive dolphins to physically extend my presence toward those dolphins who are in service. It began when I lived on O'ahu many years ago, and I felt drawn to visit the dolphins at the Kahala Hilton. They seemed very sad and sickly to me. I would find a nice place to sit down and telepath healing thoughts to them. I know intuitively (and research has proven) that when you think loving, positive thoughts and direct those thoughts to others, the recipient actually feels those thoughts and responds to them.

Many years later, when I lived in the San Diego area, I would visit the dolphins at the petting pond at Sea World. This pond was a tiny little concrete container, and it was packed with dolphins racing around to receive fish from the public. It was very disturbing to see this, but I would visit and beam them loving, healing energies.

When I visited the dolphins at the Hyatt Regency Waikoloa Resort, I was pleasantly surprised. Their dolphin facility is a two-million-gallon salt-water lagoon with depths up to twenty feet, far exceeding federal regulations for such enclosures. The six Atlantic bottle-nosed dolphins are free to swim away from the people whenever they tire of the noise and excitement.

Even though the facility looked luxurious and grand compared to some of the places dolphins end up being confined, I reminded myself that these dolphins were still in captivity. So I spent what little time I had there near the dolphin lagoon, meditating and projecting love.

I also visited the dolphins at the Mirage Resort in Las Vegas. I had heard that it was wonderful as facilities go. I had also heard there was some controversy surrounding the program. The dolphin activists were not happy with the idea that this facility was to be a permanent home for the dolphins. They preferred the concept of a halfway house. That sounded good to me! Since the fate of the dolphins and whales is inextricably tied in with that of the human species, it would benefit us all to put our efforts into living in harmony and balance together.

So it was with mixed emotions that I made a pilgrimage to the dolphins at the Mirage Resort. After paying a nominal fee, we wandered down a winding walkway and were met by a tour guide who gave a spiel about the facility and the dolphins. I don't remember what she said; I was so mesmerized by the dolphins. The incongruity of walking through a casino and past a glamorous swimming pool setting to view dolphins was just too much for me!

As if in a sleepwalk, I followed the rest of the group down below to view the dolphins from underwater windows. There appeared to be coral in the middle of the tank! I wondered if it was real or simulated. I wanted to ask how coral could grow in the middle of a tank in the desert, but I never did. I found myself mute; I was so taken with the power and the beauty of the dolphins!

My companion tugged at my sleeve to get me to pay attention to the video of baby Squirt being born in captivity, and its mother Duchess. I couldn't watch the video because I was transfixed by the dolphins in front of me. The setting was so completely unnatural, yet at the same time it was clean and attractively decorated.

The dolphins felt fine to me. I didn't pick up on any sickliness. But I didn't want to tune in on a deeper level because I knew my gut and heart would scream out to me, "Spring these dolphins! Let them experience the real coral and sea-grass. Let them feel the tides and currents. Let them flash through the water as fast as they can. Let them catch their own iridescent fish. Let them lift their heads above the ocean water and view palm trees swaying in the wind!"

I came back to reality as our group was led upstairs to observe the dolphins being put through their exercises and rewarded with fish. As I looked around at the rapt, attentive expressions of those standing with me, I realized that this event was a glimpse into the numinous and divine for them, even if they didn't realize it. Judging by the group's well-heeled appearance, their material and interpersonal needs were being met. Yet I could see in their eyes a yearning for a deeper connection to the world around them.

We live, for the most part, in a world where nobody trusts anybody anymore—not even themselves! This isolation, this distrust, causes stress. If we could just realize that dolphins are very much connected to us, we wouldn't feel so much stress.

There are long strands—seen by many who have special sight—that connect us to one another. It's possible to send out love along these connections that exist among all of us, great and small. As we do this, our hearts will lighten and our burdens will lift.

By simply acknowledging these magnificent animals, so full of life force and love, jumping around in front us, many of us could be healed of our advanced states of spiritual disease caused by separation from our spiritual core and from other people.

But how do you get the mainstream to believe that we are all connected? If only there was a technological device to demonstrate visibly those threads that connect us, that would be fabulous! In the meantime, until some genius invents this, we shall have to use our imaginations and ask for help to see and feel these connections.

Once reconnected, we'll remember what we already know in our hearts to be true (though we somehow managed to forget it with our minds). We'll start seeing every person, animal, dolphin, whale, tree, rock, and cloud as part of ourselves. The dolphins are here to help us reconnect.

How did we ever get so disconnected? According to legends and stories of many cultures, there was a momentous change that took place on this planet. Known to many as "The Fall," this event caused our planet to be quarantined and cut off from our greater galactic family. It caused us to forget. Amnesia set in, big time. Our human consciousness has been stuck in the third dimension; this is why we feel so separate and disconnected. We have been so overwhelmed by the conditioning of this third dimensional reality that we forgot who we are: multidimensional masters, just like the whales and dolphins.

The great blessing is that the cetaceans never forgot who we are, and they are reaching out to help us remember. (There are also zillions of fairies, elves, angels, elementals, and spiritual beings working hard to "jump start" our souls before it's too late.)

There *are* tremendous strides being made in the way humans view and treat dolphins. The people of Great Britain are leading the way, showing the rest of us how to do it. Most of their dolphinariums have closed. Many organizations are informing the public of the sad effects of keeping dolphins captive. They are also funding rehabilitation centers worldwide, to acclimate dolphins who have been in captivity before giving them their freedom in the ocean.

The March 1993 International Dolphin Watch newsletter happily reported: "Brazil has banned dolphinariums, and their last remaining captive, called Flipper, is being rehabilitated back into the sea. On

June 2nd, South Carolina, USA, banned the captivity of dolphins. Other aquariums such as Charleston, Monterey, and Texas have made conscious decisions not to display cetaceans."

But will we get back on track in time? Will our allies and best friends, the dolphin species, leave this planet—as many have predicted? One day, will our children come to us and ask, "Mommy, Daddy . . . what's a dolphin?"

I wish I knew. This one is a real cliffhanger. My feeling is that the jury is still out, and perhaps, if enough of us **REMEMBER,** and then reach out and help someone *else* remember, we've got a chance to awaken from this dream in time.

Chapter Eight:

The Next Adventure -
A Bedtime Teaching Tale

*All of the physical and psychological
evidence suggests that we're approaching
a crisis point in the history of the planet.
What's next?*

ONCE UPON A TIME, ON A VERY TINY BUT BRIGHT star, there gathered the Council of Twelve for a momentous meeting. The Council of Wise Ones was to determine how they would participate in a beautiful blue planet in the solar system.

After lengthy and profound deliberation, the Council decided to send their ambassadors to this planet to caretake it, until the azure planet was ready for graduation and participation with the greater universe. Thus began the involvement of the Elder Race, in the experiment of what was to become known as Planet Earth.

Upon their arrival, they discovered an abundance of emerging life forms. To expedite the evolution, the Elder Race interbred with one of the more promising life forms. Their children were the first humans. However, because the Elders were of a finer attunement, and could not withstand the dense vibrations of Earth, they left to be reharmonized with their own people.

The first humans went on to create new civilizations, sciences, and governments. Atlantis, Lemuria, and ancient Egypt were three of the great civilizations they created. Each of these civilizations was destroyed by experiments that went out of control — experiments caused by the imbalance of technology and wisdom.

Humans survived this destruction, and began again, unaware that their struggle was being observed by the Elders. The Elders waited patiently for the humans to be transformed into Beings of Light. The timetable for transformation was set.

Toward the end of the twentieth century, everyone began to see incredible changes taking place, and sensed even bigger changes in the wind. Humans with paranormal abilities began speaking about the aliens, the angels, and the illumined ones who were joining them on Earth. They knew some visitors were here to help, and some were here to hinder. Much of what was going on didn't meet the eye.

With the convergence of a multitude of energy fields increasing in intensity, humans needed much assistance. It was an intense time. Earth was going through a transition to a higher dimension, a new age, and this was the time for many humans to, at long last, realize their full potential.

The cellular memories of humans were triggered by these new energies and unseen guests. Humans started awakening. The reactions were varied.

One group became acutely aware of the environment. They were very upset over the pollution of the land and ocean, and by the destruction of many species. Rainforests were being destroyed and species were disappearing forever. They sought to stop this destruction.

Another group began to awaken through telepathic messages they received. They were told that cooperation was the key to a more harmonious transition.

Others felt drawn to leave the cities and establish rural centers. Paying heed to prophecy, they put aside provisions for the potentially scarce times ahead.

All of these groups anticipated the transformation, yet the old "program" of fear had not yet died out. The new programming of love and global consciousness was just beginning to take hold in their consciousness.

Wise ones among them spoke of the power of thought (as wise ones had before them!). They reminded the people that they had a choice. Their thoughts could create harmony or dissonance, ease or disease. Their future would be created by their thought forms.

Knowing their thoughts had power, certain groups began working together on a global scale, in an attempt to influence a harmonious emergence. They joined their hearts and minds in celebrations, and with an intensity never witnessed before.

In the midst of all this excitement, it went almost unnoticed that a new species was emerging. Genetic mutations were occurring! Some of these new beings were *very* different. They shared total telepathic rapport with each other. They could sense what the noonday heat felt like in Rio de Janeiro and what the rain felt like in London, just by tuning into each other. They had a couple of extra glands and other adaptations. They could teleport themselves wherever they wanted to go. They communicated with all the species.

While humans were busy learning the lessons they had agreed to learn (and had forgotten they had agreed to!), there were other groups that quietly and persistently held the balance for the excesses of humans. Unbeknownst to most humans, they kept the love vibration alive, even during the darkest hours on Earth. They guided these humans through the centuries, though for the most part their contributions were unrecognized.

Then came the end of the twentieth century, and human consciousness expanded enough to honor the participation of these great beings in the "Great Crazy Quilt Plan." As more and more people became aware of the loving network of great beings who were patiently assisting humans in greater evolvement, tremendous joy spread throughout the land. Humans rejoiced that they had not been abandoned and left without guidance on a big blue marble in the cosmos. They had friends to help them make the grade and graduate!

The word spread like wildfire. We have dolphin and whale friends! We have angels! We have intergalactic and multi-dimensional friends! We have a great big wonderful family!

So all of these groups pitched in to help for the final graduation. They planned a big party—just because! Earth had been one of the toughest schools in the universe, and there was going to be a graduation! We were all going Home, at last!

The End, and the Beginning . . .

 # *Postscript*

THOUGH I LIVE IN THE HAWAIIAN ISLANDS WHERE the spinner dolphin resides, I haven't seen a dolphin in a long time (except in my meditations, of course!). They don't come in toward the shoreline as frequently and visibly as the humpback whales do.

A couple of the best spots to see the dolphins are La Perouse Bay on the south shore of Maui, and near the neighboring island of Lana'i (Manele Bay), where there is reported to be a large pod.

Whales, on the other hand, are one of Maui's biggest calling cards. They are often sighted close to shore, and cause massive traffic jams and nonstop excitement when they do their balletic leaps. Tourists never tire of whale-watching, nor does it seem to get old for the locals. The whales are, quite simply, *adored* on Maui.

Like everyone else, I am just gaga over whales. I can't wait to see my first whale of the season, and I feel sad when they depart to make their seasonal journey back to Alaska. I love to go whale-watching. I can't quite figure out why I get so excited and emotional about whales. It simply isn't logical.

It's the same with dolphins. There is a heart connection that defies logical explanation.

As the years unfold, I am not surprised to see more dolphin and whale images in the news media. You see, I believe the cetaceans have a public relations program. Their desire is to feed us images, knowing that these images will trigger memories buried deep within us.

We will see more of these cetacean images as the new millennium approaches. Dolphins and whales are not a trend! Their very beingness is a wake-up call. Quite simply, the cetaceans are working to assist us to remember and fully live our soul's potential. To that end, I am part of their mission.

I had a dream recently. I saw dolphins lined up and laying parallel to the shore. As far out as I could see they were extended thus. The creature closest to the shore was not a dolphin, it was me—lined up and lying in the water just like all the other dolphins. My lucid-dreaming mind woke up in this part of the dream and analyzed its meaning. It told me that I was part of the dolphin master plan, and that I was to be a link in their long-term plans to connect our two species. Because we weren't swimming around but were firmly locked in position, body to body, my lucid-dreaming mind informed me that this was a completed design. I was to be a bridge between the dolphins and humans. I feel honored to be in this role, and very blessed to participate in this important transition!

A Message

The dolphins have asked me to convey this message to you:

Come, be with us! Your fear will melt away as you swim with us in the sea of Love.

We have much to share with you. It is not necessary to come to the ocean. Simply experience us with your heart and your imagination. We have our own unique perspective that will help you bring balance, healing, and joy into your life. We would also like you to share with us your light, your hopes and dreams. Let us unite now to bring our combined power and essence into the world, to return Earth to her former balance and glory.

Resource
Guide

Books

Anka, Darryl: ***Bashar: Blueprint For Change.*** New Solutions Publishing, Los Angeles, CA, 1990.

Burke, Terrill Miles: ***Dolphin Magic*** series. Alpha-Dolphin Press, Fiddletown, CA, Book One 1992, Book Two 1993.

Carey, Ken: ***Return of the Bird Tribes.*** Uni Sun, Kansas City, MO, 1988.

Cochran, Amanda & Callen, Karena: ***Dolphins and Their Power to Heal.*** Bloomsbury Publishing, London, England, 1992.

Doak, Wade: ***Encounters with Whales & Dolphins.*** Hodder & Stoughton, Auckland, Australia, 1981.

Dobbs, Horace: ***Dance to a Dolphin's Song.*** Jonathan Cape Ltd., London, England, 1990.

Dobbs, Horace: ***Dilo and the Call of the Deep.*** Watch Publishing, Humberside, England, 1994.

Dobbs, Horace: ***Follow a Wild Dolphin.*** Souvenir Press, London, England, 1977.

Dobbs, Horace: *Journey Into Dolphin Dreamtime.* Jonathan Cape, Ltd., London, England,1992.

Dobbs, Horace: *Magic of Dolphins.* Lutterworth Press, Guildford, England.

Dobbs, Horace: *Save the Dolphins.* Contact International Dolphin Watch.

Dobbs, Horace: *Tale of Two Dolphins.* Jonathan Cape Ltd., London, England, 1987.

Forestell, Paul & Kaufman, Gregory: *Hawaii's Humpback Whales.* Island Heritage Publishing, Aeia, HI, 1993.

Lilly, John: *Communication Between Man and Dolphin.* Julian Press, New York, NY, 1978.

Lilly, John: *Mind of a Dolphin.* Doubleday, New York, NY, 1967.

Lynch, Dudley & Kordis, Paul: *Strategy of the Dolphin.* Fawcett-Columbine, New York, NY, 1988.

McIntyre, Joan: *Mind in the Waters.* Charles Scribner & Sons, New York, NY, 1974.

McKenna, Virginia: *Into the Blue.* Aquarian Press, London, England, 1992.

McNiff, Shawn: *Art as Medicine: Creating a Therapy of the Imagination.* Shambhala Publications, Boston, MA, 1992.

Miller, Lana: *Call of the Dolphins*. Rainbow Bridge Publishing, 1989.

Monroe, Robert: *Far Journeys*. Dolphin Books, New York, NY, 1985.

Monroe, Robert: *Journeys Out of the Body*. Doubleday, New York, NY, 1971.

Mooney, Ted: *Easy Travel to Other Planets*. First Vintage Books, New York, NY, 1992.

Morgan, Elaine: *The Aquatic Ape, A Theory of Evolution*. Souvenir Press, London, England, 1982.

Nolman, Jim: *Animal Dreaming*. Bantam Books, New York, NY, 1987.

Nolman, Jim: *Dolphin Dreamtime: Talking to the Animals*. Anthony Blond, London, England, 1985.

O'Barry, Richard: *Behind the Dolphin Smile*. Algonquin Books, Chapel Hill, NC, 1988.

Ocean, Joan: *Dolphin Connection*. Dolphin Connection/Spiral Books, HI, 1989.

Oden, ViAnn: *Dialogue with a Dolphin*. Anvipa Press, Goleta, GA, 1991.

Roads, Michael J.: *Journey Into Nature*. H.J. Kramer, Inc., Tiburon, CA, 1990.

Siegel, Robert: **Whalesong.** Harper Collins, New York, NY, 1981.

Smith, Penelope: **Animal Talk.** Pegasus Publications, Pt. Reyes Station, CA, 1989.

Temple, Robert: **The Sirius Mystery.** Sidgwick & Jackson, London, England, 1976.

Wahinehookai, Rev. Jeri: **Mothership Maui: The Journey Beyond.** Papership Maui, Kihei, HI, 1991.

Williams, Heathcote: **Falling for a Dolphin.** Jonathan Cape Ltd., London, England, 1988.

Williams, Heathcote: **Whale Nation.** Jonathan Cape Ltd., London, England, 1988.

Wyllie, Timothy: **Dolphins, Extraterrestrials and Angels – Adventures Among Spiritual Intelligence.** Reprinted by Bear & Co., Santa Fe, NM, 1993.

Wyllie, Timothy: **Dolphins, Telepathy and Underwater Birthing.** Bear & Co., Santa Fe, NM, 1993.

Zukav, Gary: **Seat of the Soul.** Simon Schuster/ Fireside, New York, NY, 1990.

Tools

Dolphin Dreamtime, audiocassette to attune to
the dolphins. Available from International
Dolphin Watch, Parklands, North Ferriby,
Humberside, HU14 3ET, England.

The Dolphin Disk is a tool for connecting
and requesting attunement with dolphins.
Available from Hallie Deering, 2610
Jacks Canyon Rd., Sedona, AZ 86336.

Dolphin Meditation, audiocassette by Ashleea
Nielsen and the Dolphin Tribe – $12^{95}.
Available from Dancing Dolphin Press,
P.O. Box 959, Kihei, HI 96753-0959,
(800) 539-0203. *(See order form at end of book.)*

Hemi-Sync tapes, the Monroe Institute, Route 1,
Box 175, Faber, VA 22938, (804) 361-9132,
FAX (804) 361-1611.

The Interspecies Telepathic Connection, tape
series by Penelope Smith. Available through

Pacific Spirit Catalogue, 1334 Pacific Ave.,
Forest Grove, OR 97116, (800) 634-9057.
Also available through Pegasus Publications,
P.O. Box 1060, Point Reyes Station, CA 94956,
(415) 663-1247.

Maui Stress Buster, a beautiful gift set of relaxation
items. Includes *Maui Meditation*, a guided
visualization video, Island Essence aromatherapy body oil, Silversword Quintessentials
Flower Essence, and a shell candle – $39^{95}.
Available from Dancing Dolphin Press,
P.O. Box 959, Kihei, HI 96753-0959,
(800) 539-0203. *(See order form at end of book.)*

Mini Maui Stress Buster, a smaller version of the
above with Ashleea Nielsen's *Dolphin Meditation* audiocassette in place of the video – $29^{95}.
Available from Dancing Dolphin Press,
P.O. Box 959, Kihei, HI 96753-0959,
(800) 539-0203. *(See order form at end of book.)*

Silversword Quintessentials Flower Essences by
Cindy Johnson. An essence to enhance telepathy is available, as well as other essences
and products. Phone & FAX: (808) 572-1719,
P.O. Box 1325, Haiku, HI 96708.

Videos

Commune with the Dolphins. Available in the U.S.

The Dolphin's Touch. Available from International Dolphin Watch.

Dolphins and Orcas by Bob Talbot. Available in the U.S.

Oceania. Available from International Dolphin Watch.

Quest for the Dolphin Spirit. Available in the U.S.

Artists

Andrew Annenberg   Paula Peterson

Jean-Luc Bozzoli   Richard Pettit

Sue Dawe   Schim Schimmel

Larry DeVilbiss   Margery Spielman

Christian Riese Lassen   George Sumner

Mark MacKay   Scott Thom

Ilene Meyer   Zinnia Vita-Joosting

David Miller   Gilbert Williams

Robert Lynn Nelson   Wyland

Dale Zarrella

Music

Dolphin Dreams	by Spirit Sounds
Dolphin Dreamtime	by Glenda Lum
Dolphin Love	by Chris Michell
Into the Dreamtime	by Oceanic Tantra & Kutira Decosterd
Maui Magica	by Donny James Regalmuto
Tantric Wave	by Oceanic Tantra & Kutira Decosterd
Whales Alive!	by Paul Winter
Whales and Dolphins	by Voices of the Earth

Trips & Swims

Discover the World, The Flatt Lodge, Newcastle, Nr Carlisle, Cumbria, CA6 6PH, United Kingdom. Phone: 06977 48356.

Dolphin Connection, Joan Ocean, P.O. Box 275, Kailua, HI 96734, (808) 263-4106.

Dolphin Discovery Tour, P.O. Box 151592, San Diego, CA 92115, (619) 435-4786.

Dolphin Quest Team, Box 107, Duncan Mills, CA 95430.

Dolphin Research Center, P.O. Box 522875, Marathon Shores, FL 33052-2875, (305) 289-0002.

Dolphins Plus, A Marine Mammal and Research Center, P.O. Box 2728, Key Largo, FL 33037, (305) 451-3710.

DolphInsight, P.O. Box 4500-4499, Del Mar, CA 92014.

Dolphinswim, Rebecca Fitzgerald, P.O. Box 8653, Santa Fe, NM 87504, (505) 986-0579.

Earthwatch, 680 Mt. Auburn St., Box 403, Watertown, MA 02272.

Hyatt Regency Waikoloa, HC02 Box 5500, Waikoloa, HI 96743, (808) 885-1234.

Institute of Marine Sciences, Roatan, Bay Island, Honduras, Central America. Phone: 011 504 451327.

Kaikoura Tours, P.O. Box 89, Kaikoura, New Zealand. Phone: 0800 655 121.

Kairos, GbR, Rosa Luxemburg Str. 39, D O 1820 Belzig, Germany. Phone: 033 841 59565.

Natural Habitat Adventures, One Sussex Station, Sussex, NJ 07461, (800) 543-8197.

Oceanic Society Expeditions, Fort Mason Center, Building E, Suite E240, San Francisco, CA 94123, (415) 441-1106.

Preservation of the Amazon River Dolphin, Roxanne Kremer, 3302 N. Burton Ave., Rosemead, CA 91770, (818) 572-7273.

UNEXSO, P.O. Box 5608, Ft. Lauderdale FL 33310, (800) 992-DIVE or (305) 359-2730. *Bahamas phone number:* (809) 373-1244.

Organizations

American Cetacean Society, P.O. Box 2639,
San Pedro, CA 90731.

American Oceans Campaign, 725 Arizona Ave.,
Suite 102, Santa Monica, CA 90401.

Animal Welfare Institute, P.O. Box 3650,
Washington, D.C. 20007.

Bellerive Animal Welfare & Conservation,
P.O. Box 6, 1211 Geneva 3, Switzerland.

Cloud Nine Productions, 27 Duke Road,
Doonan via Eumundi, Q 4562 Australia.

**Coalition Against the United States Exporting
Dolphins,** 321 East Tarpon Ave., Tarpon
Springs, FL 34689.

Dancing Dolphin Institute, P.O. Box 959,
Kihei, Maui, HI 96753-0959.

The Dolphin Alliance, P.O. Box 510274,
Melbourne Beach, FL 32951.

Dolphin Database, P.O. Box 9925, College Station, TX 77842.

Dolphin Energy Club, The Monroe Institute, Rt. 1 Box 175, Faber, VA 22938-9749.

Dolphin Network, #220 Sacramento, San Francisco, CA 94115.

Dolphin Project, P.O. Box 224, Coconut Grove, FL 33233.

Earth Island Institute, 300 Broadway, Suite 28, San Francisco, CA 94133.

Earthtrust, 25 Kaneohe Bay Dr., Kailua, HI 96734.

Environmental Research & Education Foundation, 1418 Seacrest Dr., Corona del Mar, CA 92625.

Finbacks, College of the Atlantic, Bar Harbor, ME 04609 (to adopt a finback).

Friends of the Dolphins, P.O. Box 337, Thornhill, Ontario, Canada L3T4A2.

Friends of the Sea, P.O. Box 2190, Enfield, CT 06082.

Fund for Animals, 200 West 57th St., New York, NY 10019.

Graham Timmins, Seventh Wave, Dingle,
Co Kerry, Ireland.

Greenpeace, P.O. Box 96128, Washington, D.C.
20090.

The Human Dolphin Bond Project, 3 Stanhope
Place, London W2 2HP, England.

Humane Society of the U.S., 2100 L St. NW,
Washington, D.C. 20005.

*International Cetacean Education Research
Centre,* P.O. Box 110, Nambucca,
New South Wales, Australia 2448.

*International Cetacean Education Research
Centre (ICERC) Japan,* 4A, 5-3-3 Shiro-
genedai, Minato-Ku, Tokyo 108, Japan.

International Dolphin Watch, Parklands, North
Ferriby, Humberside HU14 3ET, England.

*International Wildlife Coalition (and Whale
Adoption Project),* 634 N. Falmouth Hwy,
P.O. Box 388, N. Falmouth, MA 02556.

Interspecies Communication, 273 Hidden
Meadow Lane, Friday Harbor, WA 98250.

Into the Blue, 3308 N.E. 29th Ave., Lighthouse
Point, FL 33064.

Kahua Hawaiian Institute, P.O. Box 1747, Makawao, HI 96768.

Marine Life Rescue, 12 Maylan Road, Corby, Northants NN17 2DR, England.

Marine Mammal Stranding Center, P.O. Box 773, Brigantine, NJ 08203.

Miracle Productions, P.O. Box 111, Kings Cross, Sydney, Australia NSW 2011.

The Oceania Project, P.O. Box 646, Byron Bay, Australia NSW 2481.

Orcalab, P.O. Box 258, Hanson Island, Alert Bay, VON 1A0 B.C.

One Earth Foundation, P.O. Box 968, Kailua, HI 96734.

Pacific Whale Foundation, 101 N. Kihei Rd., Kihei, Maui, HI 96753.

Port Phillip Bay Dolphin Research Project, P.O. Box 774, Rye, Victoria 3941, Australia.

Progressive Animal Welfare Society, P.O. Box 1037, Lynwood, WA 98046.

Project Interlock, Box 20, Whangarei, New Zealand.

Sea Shepherd Conservation Society, 1314 2nd St., Santa Monica, CA 90401.

Sea Watch Foundation, 7 Andrews Lane, Southwater, West Sussex, RH13 7DY, England.

SEAVISION Foundation, P.O. Box 10309, Lahaina, Maui, HI 96761.

Sierra Club Legal Defense Fund, 1531 P St. NW, Suite 200, Washington, D.C. 20005.

Whale & Dolphin Conservation Society, 191 Weston Rd., Lincoln, MA 01733.

Whales Alive Maui, P.O. Box 2058, Kihei, Maui, HI 96753.

Wild & Free, 1526 16th Ave. East, Seattle, WA 98112.

Special Projects

AquaThought Foundation. Founder David Cole
   has spent much time researching the effect on
   humans of interaction with dolphins. Aqua-
   Thought's mission is to advance understanding
   of consciousness and its relationship to healing
   and wellness.

Together, the Cancun Convention Center and
   AquaThought are developing a telepresence
   interaction system which will transport guests
   into the dolphin area of an advanced dolphin
   interaction and consciousness research facility
   (the Yucatan Interspecies Research Foundation).

Also in development is a virtual world in which
   participants are guided through world-famous
   scuba diving locations by a pod of "virtual
   dolphins." To realistically simulate dolphin
   contact, and the intense acoustic echo-location
   that dolphins often direct toward swimmers,
   AquaThought has developed neurotechnology
   which engages the participant's entire nervous
   system and sensory mechanics in the immersive
   environment.

This new technology will allow an unlimited number of participants to have the intensive and potentially healing experience of swimming with a dolphin without adversely affecting any dolphins. 22321 Susana Ave., Torrance, CA 90505, (310) 316-4563.

Dolphin Vision. David Schmidt envisions a project that utilizes the technology of IMAX SOLIDO, high-definition television, and virtual reality in conjunction with dolphin imagery to achieve the realistic effect of swimming with dolphins. 6626 Powhatan St., Riverdale, MD 20737, (301) 459-0164.

Earth Island Institute. Provides information about saving whales, commercial whaling, and how to adopt a whale. Toll-free: (800) 4-WHALES.

Paula Peterson. Offers seminars on the dolphin/human connection. P.O. Box 766, Fair Oaks, CA 95628, (916) 961-7621.

About the Author

ASHLEEA NIELSEN GRADUATED FROM A TEXAS UNI-versity with a degree in journalism. She has studied and employed many different metaphysical disciplines, including astrology, numerology, palmistry, tarot, runes, and various healing modalities.

She began communicating with dolphins in 1987, and has since conducted workshops to help others explore their dolphin connection.

Ashleea lives in Maui, Hawai'i, where she paints, writes, hikes, snorkels, and communes with the dolphins and whales.

About the Cover Artist

MARK MACKAY SEEKS TO CAPTURE "THE VERY spirit of the sea" in his paintings and sculpture. His works depict a love for the ocean and commitment to its preservation that have brought him international acclaim.

A self-taught artist, Mark's originality and attention to detail reflect the beauty, mastery, and fragility of the ocean world. Working in a variety of mediums, he has created monumental works in paint, fired ceramics, and bronze . . . from a 7'x 35' canvas painting for the Outrigger Hotels Hawai'i, to a 4,000-square-foot sculpted underwater reef in Wailea, Maui.

From his home in Maui, Mark's support of environmental organizations through his art demonstrates his dedication to the vision of a better world for all who inhabit the Earth.

YOU ARE INVITED TO SHARE YOUR DOLPHIN OR whale encounters, dreams, or adventures into Dreamtime for inclusion in Ashleea's upcoming book, *True Whale and Dolphin Stories.* Please encourage children and young people to make contributions as well!

If you are interested in future seminars, please contact Ashleea through:

Dancing Dolphin Press
P.O. Box 959
Kihei, Maui, HI 96753-0959

Dolphin Tribe. Paperback book (152 pages).

$12.95 + $3 shipping

Maui Meditation. Relaxation videotape of Maui (20 minutes). $19.95 + $3 shipping

Dolphin Meditations. Audio cassette of narrated dolphin meditations (60 minutes).

$12.95 + $2 shipping

Maui Stress Buster. Beautifully packaged gift set. Contains MADE IN MAUI items to de-stress: *Maui Meditation* videotape, Island Essence aromatherapy body oil, Silversword Quintessentials flower essences, and a seashell candle. $39.95 + $6 shipping

Mini Maui Stress Buster. Beautifully packaged gift set. Contains MADE IN MAUI items to de-stress: *Dolphin Meditations* audio cassette, Island Essence Hawaiian bath salts, Silversword Quintessentials flower essences, and a seashell candle. $29.95 + $4 shipping

Order Form

Name _____ Phone _____

Address _____

City _____ State ____ Zip _____

QTY	DESCRIPTION	COST EACH	TOTAL
		SUBTOTAL	
		SHIPPING	
		TOTAL	

Credit card orders

❏ Visa   ❏ MasterCard

_____
Credit Card Number

Expires _____

Signature _____

PHONE (800) 539-0203
FAX (808) 871-7114
or MAIL to address at right

Checks & money orders

Mail to:
DANCING DOLPHIN PRESS
P.O. BOX 959
KIHEI, MAUI, HI 96753

Booksellers, *Dolphin Tribe* is available from:

BAKER & TAYLOR
BOOKPEOPLE
BOOKLINES HAWAI'I
NEW LEAF
SAMUEL WEISER